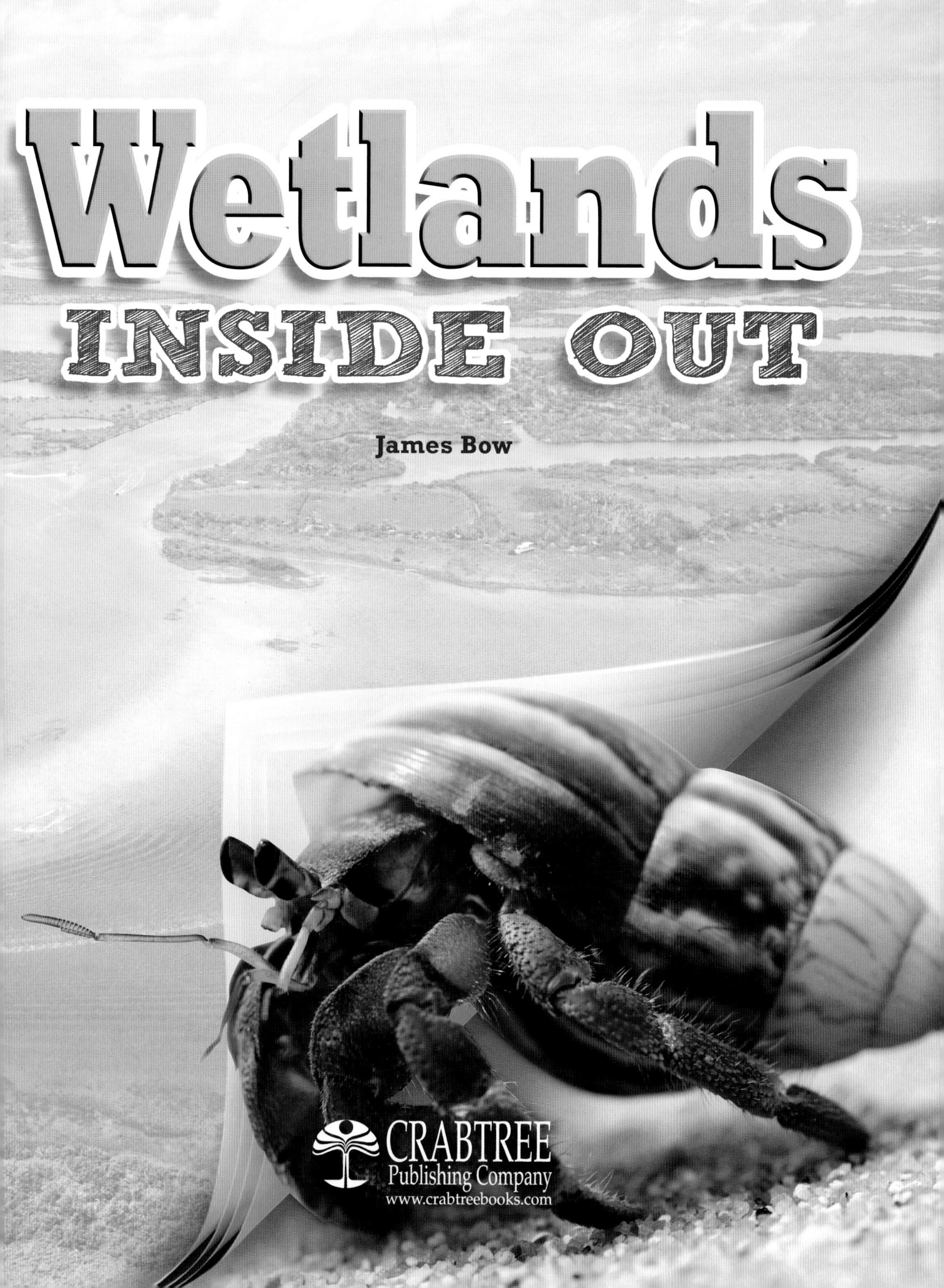

Wetlands INSIDE OUT

James Bow

CRABTREE
Publishing Company
www.crabtreebooks.com

Author: James Bow
Publishing plan research and series development: Reagan Miller
Editorial director: Kathy Middleton
Editors: Sarah Eason, Jennifer Sanderson, Nancy Dickmann, and Shirley Duke
Proofreader: Wendy Scavuzzo
Project coordinator: Sarah Eason
Design: Paul Myerscough
Photo research: Rachel Blount
Production coordinator and Prepress technician: Tammy McGarr
Print coordinator: Katherine Berti

Written, developed, and produced by Calcium

Photo Credits:

t=Top, bl=Bottom Left, br=Bottom Right

Alamy: D. Trozzo: p. 15 (br): Burns Bog Conservation Society: p. 12–13: Corbis: Serguei Fomine/Global Look: p. 18–19; Dreamstime: Bobmcleanllc: p. 14–15; Ron Chapple: p. 1, p. 16–17; Edurivero: p. 21 (bottom); Steveheap: p. 28 (b); Suebmtl: p. 8–9; Sander Van Der Werf: p. 4–5: Land Trust for the Mississippi Coastal Plain: Mark LaSalle: p. 28–29: Nature Picture Library: Vladimir Medvedev: p. 19 (tr): Shutterstock: Chbaum: p. 22–23; Defpicture: p. 11 (tr); Filipe Frazao: p. 20–21; Haveseen: p. 1 (br); Cathy Keifer: p. 13 (tr); Steve Oehlenschlager: p. 10–11 (tr); Roberto Tetsuo Okamura: p. 6–7; Jay Ondreicka: p. 17 (br); Peeradach Rattanakoses: p. 27 (br); Sorbis: p. 25 (tr); Marco Uliana: p. 23 (tr); Rudy Umans: p. 24–25; Ivonne Wierink: p. 3: Wikimedia Commons: Cephas: p. 22 (tr); Downtowngal: p. 26–27; MPF: p. 9 (tr); Shahnoor Habib Munmun: p. 10–11.

Cover: Dreamstime: Hupeng; Steveheap (br).

Library and Archives Canada Cataloguing in Publication

Bow, James, 1972-, author
Wetlands inside out / James Bow.

(Ecosystems inside out)
Includes index.
Issued in print and electronic formats.
ISBN 978-0-7787-0641-0 (bound).--
ISBN 978-0-7787-0726-4 (pbk.).--
ISBN 978-1-4271-7651-6 (pdf).--ISBN 978-1-4271-7645-5 (html)

1. Wetland ecology--Juvenile literature. 2. Wetland animals--Juvenile literature. 3. Wetland plants--Juvenile literature. I. Title.

QH541.5.M3B68 2014 j577.68 C2014-903765-1
C2014-903766-X

Library of Congress Cataloging-in-Publication Data

Bow, James.
Wetlands inside out / James Bow.
pages cm. -- (Ecosystems inside out)
Includes index.
ISBN 978-0-7787-0641-0 (reinforced library binding) --
ISBN 978-0-7787-0726-4 (pbk.) --
ISBN 978-1-4271-7651-6 (electronic pdf) --
ISBN 978-1-4271-7645-5 (electronic html)
1. Wetland ecology--Juvenile literature. 2. Wetlands--Juvenile literature. I. Title.

QH541.5.M3B68 2015
577.68--dc23

2014020969

Crabtree Publishing Company
www.crabtreebooks.com 1-800-387-7650

Printed in Hong Kong/082014/BK20140613

Published in Canada
Crabtree Publishing
616 Welland Ave.
St. Catharines, Ontario
L2M 5V6

Published in the United States
Crabtree Publishing
PMB 59051
350 Fifth Avenue, 59th Floor
New York, New York 10118

Published in the United Kingdom
Crabtree Publishing
Maritime House
Basin Road North, Hove
BN41 1WR

Published in Australia
Crabtree Publishing
3 Charles Street
Coburg North
VIC, 3058

Contents

What Is an Ecosystem?

An **ecosystem** is made up of **organisms**, the environment in which they live, and their **interrelationships**. Plants and animals need sunlight, water, air, soil, and temperatures that are not too hot or too cold. These nonliving things are called **abiotic factors**. Plants and animals also depend on each other to live. These living things are called **biotic factors**. Plants change sunlight into **energy**. Some animals eat plants, while others eat animals. They all make up a **system** in which all parts work together to survive.

How Big Are Ecosystems?

Ecosystems come in many sizes. They can be as large as an ocean, or as small as a puddle. A **biome** is a large geographical area that contains similar plants, animals, and environments. Some examples of biomes include rain forests and tundras.

What Are Wetlands?

As the name suggests, wetlands are wet lands. These are not lakes or oceans, but shallow ponds or stretches of muddy land where water soaks, or **saturates**, the ground. Although everything in a wetland is wet, it is still possible for plants to **take root** and grow. The mix of water, soil, and plant life in wetlands means there is a lot of food for animals to eat. Wetlands support a great amount of **diversity**, which means that huge numbers of different plants and animals live there.

Let's explore the different types of wetlands in the world. We will see how each ecosystem works, and look at how individual plants and animals play a key part.

What Is a System?

A system is a group of parts that work together for a purpose. Ecosystems exist because organisms could not survive without them. One plant or animal does not have everything it needs to live, so it depends on other organisms. Each abiotic and biotic factor plays an important and specific role to keep the system going. Organisms in ecosystems are **interdependent**. This means that if one organism in an ecosystem fails, the balance will be upset and affect all the other organisms in it.

This map shows where wetlands and other biomes are found around the world.

Wetlands have areas of open water and areas of wet ground. Animals have plenty to drink, and the soil provides space for plants to grow.

Energy in Ecosystems

sun

Organisms need energy. It comes from the sun, and is moved through the ecosystem as food. Animals need plants and other animals for energy. The energy, or food, network they form is called a food chain.

From Sunlight to Sugar

Every food chain includes three types of organisms. Producers are the first part of a food chain. These are plants and **algae** that use **chlorophyll** to make their own food from the sun through a process called **photosynthesis**.

Next in the food chain are the consumers. Herbivores eat plants for energy, and carnivores eat the animals that eat plants. Animals that eat plants and animals are called omnivores.

The final step in the food chain is the decomposers. Tiny organisms, such as **fungi** and **bacteria**, eat dead plants and animals, breaking them down and returning **nutrients** to the soil. When the plants take up the nutrients, the food chain begins again.

The Food Web

The food chain is a simple model of what happens in nature. Most organisms eat many **species**, not just one, so you can picture this as a **food web** made of interlinking food chains. A healthy food web has many different plants and animals, and this variety of organisms is called **biodiversity**.

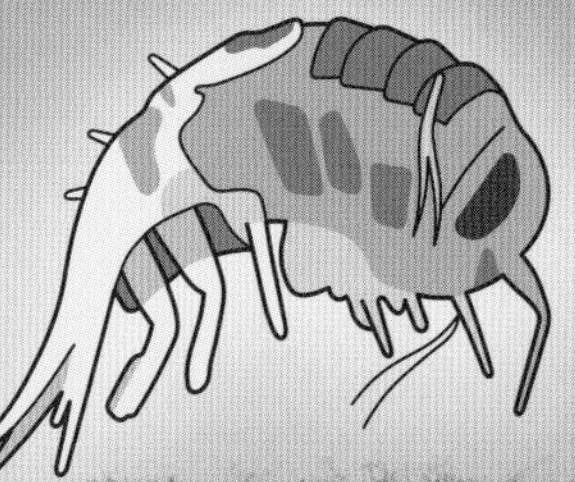

This food chain shows the flow of energy from one organism to another.

Eco Up Close

Chlorella is a type of algae that is often called pond scum. Algae are organisms that are different from both plants and animals. Although very small, pond scum **reproduces** in great numbers, and it can cover the surface of large ponds. It has chlorophyll that changes sunlight to energy, stored as sugar, through photosynthesis. Pond scum is full of the nutrients and energy organisms need. It is an important food for insects, small fishes, and oysters. Pond scum is the bottom of the food chain, and it provides food for many wetland organisms that would go hungry without it.

Alligators are at the top of the food chain in the wetlands where they live.

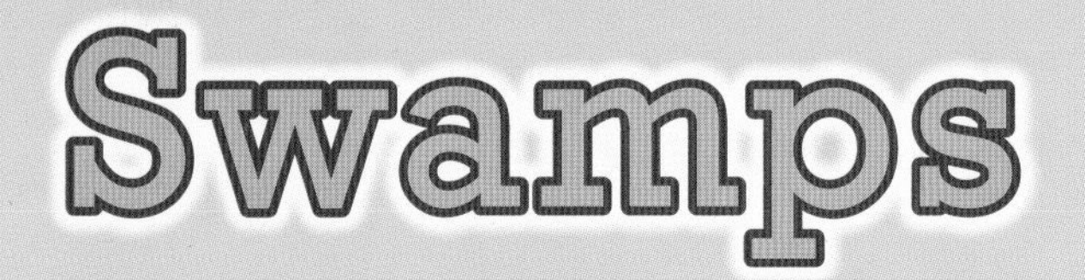

Different wetlands have different names. Their name depends on where the wetland's water comes from or what grows in it. Swamps are one of the best-known wetlands. Water from lakes or streams runs, or drains, into swamps. Swamps have many different types of plants, especially trees. These wetlands are often described as dark, dangerous, and smelling of rotting plants. However, swamps provide important habitats for fish, insects, amphibians, and reptiles, as well as some birds and mammals.

Although the leaves and flowers of waterlilies float on the surface of the water, the plant's roots reach into the soil at the bottom of the pond.

Wooded Paradise

The Beverly Swamp is found in Canada. This 6,000-acre (2,428-ha) swamp is found near the city of Hamilton, Ontario. Pure water from cold springs run into three **watersheds**, which then drain into Lake Erie and Lake Ontario. The swamp is one of the largest wetlands with forests in southern Ontario. It has many species of trees, ferns, grasses, and wildflowers. These feed mustard white butterflies, white-throated sparrows, the rare pickerel frog, and the northern flying squirrel. The swamp provides shelter, clean water, and food for many different organisms that either live in the swamp or visit it.

Eco Focus

Although the Beverly Swamp is found near a large **urban area** in North America, 114 landowners protect much of the swamp. They have agreed not to build on or near it. What could happen to the wetland if this changes and people build closer to the swamp? Explain your thinking.

Eco Up Close

The black spruce **thrives** in wet soil, and can be found in most swamps in northeastern North America. It grows to a height of 45 feet (14 m), and it grows best in cool, **temperate climates**.

The spruce is a pioneer species. A pioneer species is one of the first species to arrive in an area. As the spruce grows on the wet soil, it shades the water and its fallen needles add nutrients to the soil. Eventually, this allows other trees to grow, turning an **open marsh** into a wet forest.

black spruce

Ponds and Marshes

If trees are removed from swamps, a pond or a marsh is left. Without an umbrella, or canopy, of leaves to block the sun, sunlight reaches the water's surface. This allows reeds and water grasses to grow. Marshes provide excellent habitats for birds that travel, or migrate, there. Waterbirds such as ducks and geese often travel from one marsh to the next, where the birds can rest, swim, and eat before moving on again.

An Important Breeding Ground

The Delta Marsh in southern Manitoba, Canada, is one of the largest **freshwater** marshes in the world. The marsh is made up of a number of bays on the southern shore of Lake Manitoba. The bays stretch over 18 miles (29 km) and are separated from the lake by a long, forested sand dune. The bays extend more than 2.5 miles (4 km) south from Lake Manitoba's shore.

The Delta Marsh is an important stop for many migrating birds. These include Canada geese, snow geese, and mallard ducks. The birds rest on the marsh and find food before continuing their journey to their summer or winter **nesting grounds**. The birds feed on the many insects that live in the marsh. The Delta Marsh is also home to deer and beavers, as well as **predators**, such as foxes and coyotes.

The open water of a marsh provides geese, ducks, and other birds with food and the chance to rest during their migrations. It also makes it more difficult for predators to sneak up on and attack them.

dragonfly

Eco Up Close

The dragonfly is one of more than 100,000 insects found in the world's wetlands. It is one of the largest wetland insects, and is also a predator. Dragonflies eat mosquitoes. By doing so, they keep mosquito numbers from growing out of control. Dragonflies need open water to lay their eggs. Dragonfly **larvae** stay underwater until they grow into adults. They provide food for other marsh creatures, such as fish, frogs, and birds.

Bogs and Fens

In some places, water does not run, or drain, into a stream or lake. Instead, it stays still. In these places, a mire forms. Another name for a mire is muskeg. There are two types of mires: bogs and fens. Bogs are mires fed by rain or underground springs. Fens are low areas where water from streams gets in, but cannot easily get out.

Low on Oxygen

The waters of bogs and fens have very little **oxygen** and few nutrients. This makes them difficult places for fish to live or plants to grow. As difficult as the conditions are, there is life. Some plants, such as moss, cranberries, and certain blueberries, grow well in bogs. These plants have tough, woody stems that can **filter** water and make the most of the few nutrients within it. The plants that grow in bogs and fens provide food for herbivores, such as beavers, caribou, and moose. Bears and wolves in turn feed on these herbivores.

Burns Bog is the one of the largest bogs in North America. It stretches across 15 square miles (39 sq km) in Delta, British Columbia, 16 miles (26 km) southeast of Vancouver. It provides a home for more than 50 species of mammals and 200 species of birds. Black bears have also been seen in the bog.

Low oxygen levels in bogs means that few decomposers can survive there. This helps keep dead plants and animals from rotting. Wood, skeletons, and even tools from thousands of years ago have all been found in bogs.

sundew

Eco Up Close

In bogs and other wetlands with low nutrients, plants sometimes get their nutrients from other sources. The drosera, also known as the sundew, is a meat-eating plant that grows in Burns Bog. Sundews grow long stalks with sweet, sticky spikes that attract insects. When an insect lands on the plant, the stalk rolls up around the insect. The plant oozes special juices to **digest** the insect. Other meat-eating plants include the pitcher plant and the Venus flytrap.

Estuaries

Rivers drain into oceans, and an estuary can form where the two bodies of water meet. Here, the sediments are stirred up as the waters mix. River water flows into estuaries, bringing them fresh water. Tides and waves move the sediments such as dirt, sand, and soil on the riverbeds, which form a sheltered area. They also bring salt water from the sea to the estuary. Estuary waters are full of nutrients for plants and animals.

Busy Places

Chesapeake Bay, between Virginia and Maryland, is the largest estuary in the United States. There, water from 150 streams and rivers drains into the bay. The tides move the water, shifting sediment and changing the salinity (how salty things are) and oxygen levels. This makes good conditions for clams and oysters. They sit on the bottom of the estuary and let the waters bring them food, such as plankton.

Many fish and birds depend on estuaries, feeding off their plankton and insects. The fish and birds become food for predators, such as seals, whales, and sharks. The amount of food found around estuaries has also attracted people, who have built cities there. However, the cities bring pollution, which threatens the very ecosystems that brought people to the area in the first place.

Eco Focus

Of the 32 largest cities in the world, 22 are built on estuaries. What draws people to these places? What conditions might put all the life in those locations at risk? Explain your thinking.

The dirt and sand carried by rivers is often dropped at an estuary. This helps create sandy, **fertile** soil for plants.

Eco Up Close

The oyster thrives in estuaries such as Chesapeake Bay. Oysters also provide food for seabirds and otters. Otters use rocks to break oyster shells to get at the oysters' soft insides. Oysters eat everything that comes their way, including **pollutants**. This affects the other animals that eat the oysters. Pollution and **overfishing** have reduced the Chesapeake Bay oyster population to less than 1 percent of what it was before the 1800s.

oyster

Tidal Flats and Salt Marshes

The Moon pulls at our planet. Its gravity can raise the level of the ocean beneath it by as much as 3 feet (1 m). This movement makes tides where the ocean meets the land. At high tide, water moves up the land, flooding beaches and low-lying areas. At low tide, the water slips away, leaving pools of salt water behind. These wetlands are called tidal flats and salt marshes.

A Salty Meal

The water in tidal flats and salt marshes is salty, so organisms must **adapt** to live there. The marshes of the Louisiana coast are covered in **salt-resistant** grasses. Salt- resistant means not affected by salt. The grasses provide a home for small ocean-living animals. These include baby shrimp, redfish, and sea-trout, as well as a number of insects. These animals, in turn, attract birds and provide food for reptiles such as turtles. Predators found in tidal flats and salt marshes include crocodiles and herons.

The plants in a salt marsh keep the soil from being washed away by the tides. Salt marshes provide a barrier between the ocean and the freshwater ecosystems found inland.

Tidal flats can be huge areas that stretch for miles.

Eco Up Close

The diamondback terrapin is a turtle that has adapted to live in salt marshes. Its skin is not affected by salt and it has **webbed** hind feet to help it swim. The terrapins can also taste the difference between salt water and drinkable fresh water. The fact that they can survive in salt water means they can live where freshwater turtles cannot, which reduces the terrapins' competition for food.

diamondback terrapin

The West Siberian Plain

The largest wetland in the world is the West Siberian Plain. It is stretches across more than 1.05 million square miles (2.72 million sq km) of land. It covers an area in north central Russia as large as Alaska, Texas, and California put together. The area is low, flat, and hard to drain, so it has many bogs, fens, swamps, and marshes. Stretching 1,500 miles (2,414 km) from north to south, this wetland has many different climates. In the south, there are swamps, marshes, and warm flooded grasslands. In the north, there is muskeg and tundra.

Largest Swamp

The West Siberian Plain contains the Vasyugan Swamp, which is the largest swamp in the **northern hemisphere**. It has cold winters and short summers. It is home to pine, spruce, and cedar trees, which thrive on the wet soil. Many different insect species, such as butterflies and beetles, live in the swamp. These insects provide food for salamanders, frogs, and toads. The larger predators that live in the swamp include lynx and brown bears.

Altogether, 195 species of birds visit the swamp. The rich landscape, with areas of open water and sheltered areas, is perfect for hunting and nesting.

Siberian salamander

The West Siberian Plain is so large that in its northernmost part is a tundra wetland and its southernmost part has flooded grasslands. Wetlands can be found as parts of other biomes that have the conditions needed for wetlands to form.

Eco Up Close

Salamanders thrive in wetlands. The Siberian salamander lays its eggs in water, and the young salamanders swim and breathe water through **gills**. As they get older, they grow lungs that breathe air. Then they leave the water. The Siberian salamander has also adapted to the cold conditions of northern Russia. It is able to freeze underground for years before **thawing** and walking away unharmed! Salamanders eat insects and are eaten by larger predators, such as herons.

The Pantanal

The Pantanal wetland in South America is a floodplain that floods during the rainy season. It covers at least 54,000 square miles (139,859 sq km) of Brazil, Bolivia, and Paraguay. The huge floodplain has many different biomes. Tropical rainforest plants, semiarid woodland plants, and grasses all live close to one another.

Pantanal

An Explosion of Life

The Pantanal is one of the most diverse places on the planet. It contains more than 3,500 species of plants, 100 species of mammals, and 650 species of birds. It also has almost 100 species of reptiles, and more than 300 species of fish and 40 species of amphibians. There are millions of insects, too. This huge food web includes plants such as reeds, grasses, and trees. The plants provide food and shelter for many animals, which provide food for more animals. With so much biodiversity, it is difficult to imagine how the ecosystem could be harmed.

The Pantanal has a variety of plant species, all of which provide food for many of its wetland animals.

However, if the conditions of an ecosystem are changed, the plants and animals within it are affected. Farmers draining wetlands rob plants of water, which then robs animals of food and shelter. Changes at the ecosystem's center ripple across the food web and have a major impact.

Eco Up Close

The marsh deer is the largest deer species of South America. Its numbers have been reduced to just a few **populations** in marshy zones such as the Pantanal. Though hunting and habitat loss have made their main predators, such as the jaguar, almost completely disappear, the marsh deer is still threatened by people. The deer are hunted for their antlers, and their habitat is drained to make way for farmland. The deer also catch diseases from farm cattle.

marsh deer

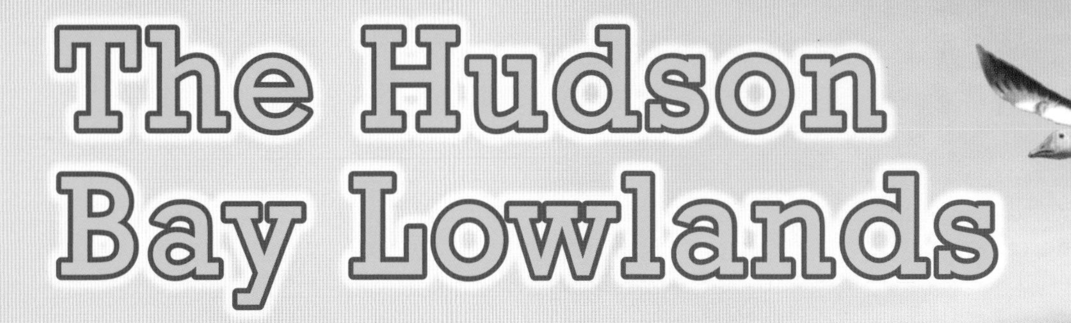

The Hudson Bay Lowlands

The Hudson Bay Lowlands are the low-lying lands along the coast of Hudson Bay and James Bay in northwestern Quebec, northern Ontario, and northeastern Manitoba. Water from several slow-moving rivers, as well as water from the bays themselves, runs into the lowlands. At more than 186,000 square miles (481,738 sq km), the lowlands make up the largest wetland in North America.

Hudson Bay Lowlands

Icebound

The Hudson Bay Lowlands are so far north that they have long, cold winters. During these winter, the rivers and bays of the lowland freeze. However, the animals that live in the lowlands have adapted to these conditions. Herbivores such as caribou can travel for hundreds of miles (kilometers) to find food. Polar bears and other predators can walk on the ice and follow them. In the summer, the lowlands' many swamps, bogs, estuaries, and tidal flats melt. Then the trees and wildflowers **bloom** with an explosion of food, which brings out insects and migrating birds. Even if a wetland is frozen for months, it is still a wetland.

Over the course of a year, the Hudson Bay Lowlands have features found in two different ecosystems: the watery conditions of wetlands and the icy conditions of a tundra.

Eco Up Close

In just one season, the Hudson Bay Lowlands are home to millions of mosquitoes, along with black flies and midges. These insects bite animals, including people, and feed off their blood. They can also pass diseases to people and animals. To stop this, people tried killing the insects with poisons. This polluted the ecosystem. By killing the insects, it also meant that less food was available for birds and insects such as dragonflies.

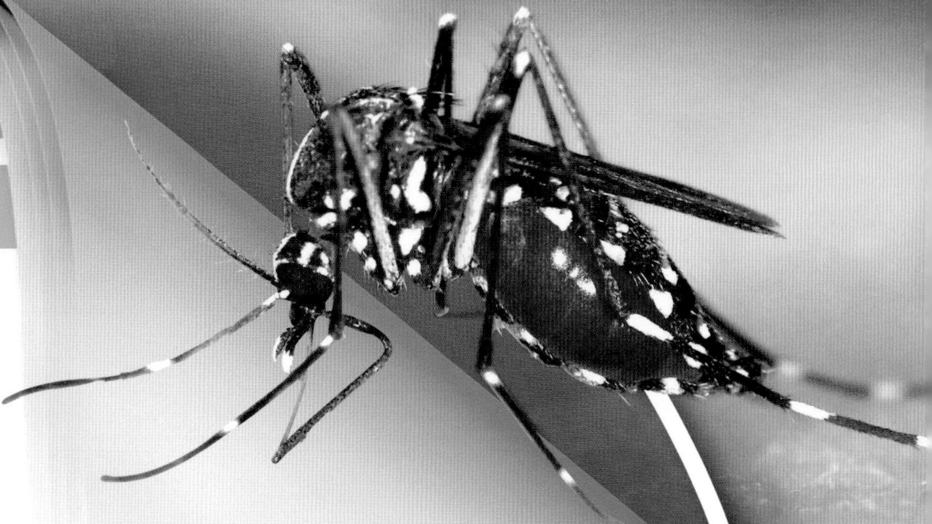

mosquito

The Florida Everglades

The Florida Everglades are North America's largest flooded grassland. From May to October, heavy rain turns the Everglades into a slow-moving river that is 60 miles (97 km) wide and 100 miles (161 km) long.

Full of Life

Sawgrass fills much of the Everglades. This plant grows so thick that it is almost impossible to walk through, but alligators can make nests among it. The Everglades are not just flooded grasslands. Drier areas have pine, mangrove, and cypress trees. These provide homes for fish, turtles, snakes, and birds, which feed on the many insects.

Wild alligators are found only in the United States and China, while crocodiles can be found in tropical wetlands around the world. Alligators have a wide u-shaped snout, whereas crocodiles have a narrow v-shaped snout.

Fire on the Water

Fire is an important abiotic factor in the Everglades. Lightning from thunderstorms starts fires, which help pine trees and sawgrass. The bark of the pine tree is thick, so it is protected from the fire. However, the flames open up the tree's pinecones. This releases their seeds, which then grow. The fire burns only the part of sawgrass that grows above the water. Its roots are safe beneath the water, so the plant survives. However, the fire burns away other plants that compete with sawgrass. This gives the plant a huge advantage.

Eco Focus

In the 1930s, attempts to control flooding in the Everglades dried out parts of the wetland. Then people discovered salty ocean water was seeping into the wells of the nearby city of Miami. How could these two events be connected? Explain your thinking.

Eco Up Close

Alligators are the **apex predator** of the Everglades. They can grow up to 15 feet (4.6 m) long and weigh as much as 1,000 pounds (454 kg). They swim just below the surface of the water with only their snout in the air, allowing them to breathe. They sneak up on their **prey** before lunging to bite it and carry it underwater. Alligators are cold-blooded animals that use the warmth of their surrounding environment to heat their bodies, so they thrive in the warm waters of the Everglades. In the summer, they lay their eggs in nests that they build on land.

Artificial Wetlands

People have only recently discovered how very important wetlands are. Wetlands filter dirt and pollutants from water. They slow down the movement of rainwater and protect areas from flooding because plants slow the water's speed and absorb and store some of the extra water. The many plants found in wetlands take in, or absorb, carbon dioxide from the air and return it to the soil. Carbon dioxide is a greenhouse gas. By absorbing the gas, wetlands help reduce climate change.

Building Our Own Wetlands

People have worked hard to restore wetlands. Removing drains and dikes allows water to flow to wetlands naturally. Stopping people from hunting protects the animals living there. Building wetlands in urban areas keeps water cleaner and prevents flooding. Wetlands created in cities are urban habitats for wetland life.

Wetlands have even been brought indoors. "Living walls" are mini wetlands built indoors. Plants and small animals such as fishes provide food for each other and help clean the water and the air. These wetlands are teaching tools that show us how all species in an ecosystem depend on one another to survive.

Urban wetlands help provide cities with clean water and natural green spaces for people to enjoy.

Eco Focus

Heavy rainfall in urban areas often results in uncontrollable water on the ground, called runoff. How can wetlands be used to control water runoff in your neighborhood? Explain your thinking.

Eco Up Close

"Green roofs" are another way to use the tools of nature to create cities that are better for the environment. By creating gardens on top of buildings, the flow of rainwater through city sewer systems is slowed. The amount of carbon dioxide and other pollutants is also reduced. Green roofs save energy by providing insulation in winter and absorbing less heat from sunlight in summer. They also attract and provide homes for birds and insects in our cities.

green roof

The Wetland Is the Best Land

Wetlands are areas of great biodiversity, sources of oxygen, and absorbers of carbon dioxide. They clean our water and protect us from floods. They can create valuable green spaces for our cities. In spite of our improved understanding of wetlands, many are still under threat. Pollution is poisoning the food chain in many wetland ecosystems. Hunting has brought many wetland species to extinction. We need to clean up and restore damaged wetlands.

What Can You Do?

Write to politicians to tell them about the need to protect wetlands. Encourage city leaders to restore or create new wetlands in urban areas.

Volunteer with groups that work to preserve natural areas. Help clean up the natural areas where you live.

Save energy and reduce your water use. Walk, bicycle, or use public transportation instead of using a car.

Most importantly, educate yourself. Where are the wetlands nearest to you? What can you do to help protect them?

Activity:

Create Your Own Wetland!

Discover for yourself what happens when a wetland is allowed to thrive.

You Will Need:

- Shallow pan
- Two large sponges
- Watering can
- Clay
- Potting soil

Instructions

1. Make a hill out of the clay on one side of the pan. Make sure this hill slopes down toward the middle.
2. Place the sponges next to the clay in the middle of the pan. These represent the wetland. The rest of the pan represents a lake.
3. Sprinkle potting soil over the clay.
4. Using the watering can, slowly pour water over the highest part of the clay. Observe what happens.

The Challenge

Once your experiment is complete, present it to others and discuss the following questions:

- How long did it take the water to flow into the "lake"?
- What effect did the wetland sponges have?
- What happened to the dirt sprinkled on the clay?
- Did all the dirt end up in the lake?

Try this experiment again without the wetland sponges.

wetland

Glossary

Please note: Some bold-faced words are defined in the text

abiotic factors Nonliving parts of an ecosystem, such as water and soil
adapt To change over long periods of time or many generations to better survive an environment
algae A group of organisms that have chlorophyll and can make their own food, but are not plants
amphibians Animals, such as frogs and salamanders, that begin life in water, then live on land as adults
apex predator An animal at the top of the food chain, which has few, if any, predators of its own
bacteria Living organisms made up of one cell
biodiversity The variety of plant and animal life in an ecosystem or other area on Earth
biotic factors Living parts of an ecosystem, such as plants and animals
bloom To grow flowers
canopy Tree branches with leaves forming the upper layer of a forest
chlorophyll A green substance in plants that changes sunlight and carbon dioxide into energy, which is stored as sugar and used by the plant for food
climate change A process in which the environment changes to become warmer, colder, drier, or wetter than normal. This can occur naturally, or it can be caused by human activity
climates The normal weather in specific areas
digest To extract nutrients from food
diversity Having many different types of something
ecosystem A group of living and nonliving things that live and interact in an area
energy The power that nutrients from food provide to the body
extinction The dying out of a species
fertile Having or capable of producing an abundance of vegetation
filter To remove substances from a liquid
floodplain A stretch of land around a river onto which the river floods
food chain A chain of organisms in which each member uses the member below as food
food web The interlinked food chains in an ecosystem
freshwater Describing something made from or containing water that does not contain salt
fungi A kind of organism that absorbs food
gills The body parts fish and some amphibians use to breathe.
grassland Areas where grasses are the main form of plant life
gravity A pulling force that acts on objects
greenhouse gas Additional gases in the air, such as carbon dioxide or methane, which trap the sun's heat in the atmosphere and keep it from being reflected out into space
habitats The natural environments of animals and plants
interdependent Relying on each other for survival
interrelationships The relationships between many different organisms and their environment
larvae The young, wingless, feeding stage of insects
mammals Warm-blooded animals that have lungs, a backbone, and hair or fur, and drink milk from their mother's body
migrate To travel to another area for food or to reproduce
nesting grounds Places where birds build their nests and raise their young
northern hemisphere Land that is north of the equator
nutrients Substances that allow organisms to thrive and grow
open marsh An area of wetland that is mostly water with no plants.

organisms Living things
overfishing Taking too many fish for food
oxygen A gas found in air that organisms need for breathing
photosynthesis The process in which plants use sunlight to change carbon dioxide and water into food and oxygen
pollutants Chemicals or other substances that are dirty and harmful
populations The total numbers of species in an area
predators Animals that hunt other animals for food
prey An animal that is hunted by another animal for food
reproduces Produces offspring
reptiles Animals, such as lizards and snakes, that have scales and that rely on the surrounding temperature to warm or cool their bodies
saturates Is so full of water it cannot absorb any more
sediments Dirt, sand, or soil that is carried away by fast-moving water and which falls to the bottom of a body of water when the flow slows down
semiarid Not dry enough to be a desert
species A group of animals or plants that are similar and can produce young
take root To grow roots into the soil
temperate A temperature that is not too hot and not too cold
thawing The melting of ice
thrives Grows and stays healthy
tides The regular rise and fall of ocean water
tropical Describing a hot and humid climate
urban area A town or city
watersheds Areas of land that are drained by a single river, lake, or stream
webbed Having toes or fingers connected by a membrane of skin

Learning More

Find out more about Earth's precious wetland ecosystems.

Books

Gray, Susan Heinrichs. *Ecology: The Study of Ecosystems*. New York: Scholastic, 2012.

Schomp, Virginia. *24 Hours in the Wetlands (A Day in an Ecosystem)*. New York: Cavendish Square Publishing, 2013.

Sill, Cathryn *Wetlands*. Atlanta, GA: Peachtree, 2013.

Websites

Learn more about ecology and how you can help care for the planet at:
www.ecology.com/ecology-kids

Find out more about wetland ecosystems at:
http://kids.nceas.ucsb.edu/biomes/freshwaterwetlands.html

Learn more about wetlands, how they are formed, and the plants and animals that live there at:
www.nwf.org/Kids/Ranger-Rick/Animals/Mixture-of-Species/What-Is-A-Wetland.aspx

Find out how you can join projects that could kick-start your ecology career at:
www.kidsecologycorps.org

Index